Kate Liberty

Freshwater Aquariums

A Complete Guide to Take Care of Your Aquarium Fish.

Basics, Set Up, Keeping, Maintenance

Table of Contents

Introduction

If you're looking for an easy way to enjoy the beauty of the underwater world in your own home, a freshwater aquarium might be just the thing for you. Freshwater aquariums feature fish, plants, and other animals that live in freshwater lakes, rivers, and streams.

An aquarium is a tank or an artificial pond where fish, plants, and other aquatic organisms are kept. Fish keepers use this aquatic habitat to keep fish, plants, and invertebrates for their enjoyment, for shelter, or to study their behavior. There are freshwater and marine aquariums. They have become popular in recent decades with the availability of specialized equipment such as heaters and filters.

A freshwater aquarium is a type of vivarium made to house freshwater aquatic animals. The term generally refers to a tank or an aquarium with liquid and solid materials. Freshwater fish are often sold as food for larger fish, reptiles, or amphibians.Freshwater aquariums are a fun and rewarding hobby. Knowing how to set one up, however, can be a little confusing. This guide will get you started and help you choose the right freshwater fish for your aquarium.

A freshwater aquarium can be a good choice for those looking to get into the fish keeping hobby. The freshwater aquarium is a simpler type of aquarium to maintain and keep running than saltwater aquariums. Freshwater aquariums also tend to be more affordable than saltwater aquariums. However, some challenges come with keeping freshwater fish.

The freshwater aquarium is the most common type of aquarium. A freshwater aquarium is an enclosure that holds water and aquatic plants, with fish or other aquatic animals. It can be contrasted with a saltwater aquarium, which similarly holds water and aquatic plants but has marine animals. Both aquariums can have tropical or cold-water fish, invertebrates, plants, algae, or other aquatic life. Freshwater tanks have some very specific issues when it comes to maintaining them.

Freshwater fish are being kept in aquariums all over the world for several reasons. Their beauty and grace is part of the reason why many people love to have them as pets. Freshwater aquarium fish are also easy to care for as long as you know what exactly to do. It also doesn't hurt that there is a wide variety of freshwater fish to choose from. Fishkeeping has become one of the most popular hobbies across the globe. Whether you're a complete beginner or an oldhand at keeping fish, Freshwater Aquarium: Everything You Need to Know to Keep a Healthy Fish Tank is the book for you. It's full of expert advice on everything from picking the right aquarium for you and your fish to setting it up, maintaining it, and stocking it with everything from the tiniest baby fish to large adult fish.

An aquarium is a water-filled enclosure at least partially with fish or plants. Multiple words have been used in English to describe a receptacle for holding fish. The term "aquarium" was coined by Philip Gosse, a naturalist in British marine zoology, when he published the book "The Aquarium: An Unveiling of the Deep Sea Wonders" 1854.

A freshwater aquarium is a type of aquarium filled with freshwater and kept under ambient temperature conditions (instead of a cold-water aquarium). Freshwater fishkeeping has become popular among hobbyists since the 1970s, and by the turn of the century, it had become one of the most popular types of aquaria for fish.

If you're thinking of starting an aquarium but have never set up one before, you'll be happy to know that the job can be done with very little experience. With the right information, you'll be able to create a beautiful freshwater or saltwater aquarium that will look great and add an interesting focal point to any room in your home.

It's always an exciting moment when you begin to set up your first aquarium. Your fish tank can be the perfect place for you to slow down, relax, and escape from your busy life. However, setting up a freshwater aquarium requires a lot of hard work and dedication.

The Aquarium

The aquarium is considered a masterpiece, be it in a home or public place. So, before selecting the type of aquarium size shape, it is essential to make the following considerations:

- The space available
- The cost
- The types of aquarium fish you would love to keep.

The type and number of fish you are planning is a good gauge to determine the aquarium you require. Choosing the aquarium of the appropriate size would prevent overstocking of the fish. So, whatever the size of the aquarium you may choose, it is alwaysgood practice overstocking. Since it would inhibit and harm your fishes and may lead to an increase in mortality rates.

Getting Ready for Purchase

Once you have determined the type of fishes and the size of the aquarium, the next you would want to do is fix a budget for the aquarium setup. From our vast experience, we could say that you would be amazed by the quantity and variety of equipment available in the market.

So, we would recommend making a list of the equipment that you would require before heading

for the purchases. Here's an equipment list that Freshwater Aquarium setup would ideally have :

- Aquarium (Fish Tank)
- Filter (With Filter Media) — Check out the Top Canister Filters here
- Air-Pump (For Aeration)
- Gravel (Substrate Materials)
- Decor (Aquascaping)
- Aquarium Heater
- Lighting — Check out some of the industry-preferred Freshwater Lighting here
- Aquarium Thermometer
- Aquarium Gravel Vacuum Cleaner
- Aquarium Glass Scrubber
- Aquarium Fish Net
- Aquarium Water Test Kits
- Soft Sponge
- Bucket

Benefits of Aquarium

1. Reduce Stress Levels:

Stress has, unfortunately, become a standard part of our life. From high-schoolers to retirees, almost everyone feels the stress of some kind. One of the best ways to reduce stress and blood pressure is working on and looking at an aquarium.

Keeping an aquarium has been clinically proven to be associated with relaxation.

The reason why aquarium can help keep stress levels has to do with both water and fish. The relaxing water movement and fish lazily swimming about (or darting here and there, if it's an active species) provides us with a primal sense of peace, something that quieter waterfalls tend to do as well.

Focusing inhabitants of the fish tank also help people mentally unwind and become less stressed.

Creating and managing an aquarium is also found to reduce the stress level. A thriving home aquarium gives you a sense of accomplishment, and maintaining your aquarium requires you to spend some time daily observing working your fish.

This doesn't only distract you from whatever is stressing you, but staying close to a calmaquarium environment puts your mind at ease. It's one of the reasons you may find an aquarium in a doctor's waiting room — It helps reduce the stress of waiting.

2. Lowers Heart Rate and Blood Pressure

Advantages of aquaria tanks goes psychology and you can actually experience physiological improvements, by watching an aquarium. A study conducted by Plymouth researches revealed that watching reduced blood pressure and heart rate. The study was conducted in a controlled environment. It was found that the more biologically diverse the aquarium is, the more it impacts the blood pressure and heart rate of participants of the study.

While it hasn't been replicated exactly for home settings, it can be inferred that the physiological benefits of a fish tank (like lower blood pressure), especially one that is rich in biodiversity, might be the same in a home as well.

Though a point of contention here is the element you feel responsible for the fish in your home aquarium. And if you see fin-nippers tank attacking the beautiful Betta, you just put in, or some tank inhabitants are savaging your beautiful fish tanks plants, your heart rate not stay down.

But that happens when aquarists are not careful about stocking and tank maintenance. Most aquarists relish seeing a thriving tank, and a healthy tank with happy fish is definitely good for your health as well.

3. Decreased Pain and Anxiety

It has been known for ages that many animals have an anxiety-reducing effect on humans (not wild lions or mosquitos maybe). A study was conducted, and it was found that people in a controlled group that interacted and worked with pet fish, saw by 58.2% average. The same study highlighted the anxiety-reducing effect of plants as well, and that means you can compound the calming effects by keeping a fish tank with plants.

While pet fish can't help you with pain if you fell down the stairs or broke a nail, but it can help with pain caused by stress or anxiety.

High blood pressure usually causes headaches, and observing a fish tank can help alleviate that pain. Similarly, and stress often manifest in headaches and pains, and by reducing stress levels and your pet fish can actually improve your health.

4. Aquarium Fish Have Calming Effects

While lowering blood pressure and heart rate relates to a person calming down, there are other ways that aquarium fish have calming effects as well. A person might feel agitated or disturbed for a variety of reasons. One of the ways psychologists recommend for calming down in such a situation is finding internal and external triggers.

And watching aquarium fish is one of the best external triggers, due inherent calming effects. The benefit is especially pronounced for individuals with pet allergies, that can't interact with other pets. And since fish are "social distancing" pets, observing them can calm people down.

5. Improving Alzheimer's Patients

Multiple studies have been conducted on people with Alzheimer's and one of the advantages of aquarium. It has been observed that Alzheimer's patients, who were exposed to fish tanks, showed less disruptive behavior and consumed more food.

The benefit is attributed to the calming effect that an aquarium and fish have on people, and made Alzheimer's patients who are either too distracted or agitated to eat their food normally (and have to be provided with nutritional supplements) consumed 20% to 25% more food when in close proximity of an aquarium.

6. Improve Your Quality of Sleep

A calm mind isn't just imperative forour health, but also ourquality of sleep. A mind many thoughts rarely allows for a good night's sleep, and that's where a fish tank comes in. One of the fish tank benefits is it can help you relax and calm down. Instead of counting sheep, observing fish in your fish tank has a significantly better chance of assisting you with peaceful and deep sleep.

How to Assemble a Freshwater Aquarium

This is the fun part: the actual aquarium assembly! And we are one step closer to adding our aquatic friends. First, look at the equipment to build our freshwater aquarium. Next, check out some optional products. Finally, find a list of necessary test kits.

Setting Up Your Freshwater Aquarium

Equipment:

- Aquarium
- Aquarium Stand
- Top and Light
- Filter
- Heater
- Thermometer
- Power Strip
- Background
- Gravel
- Decorations
- Water Conditioner
- Bacteria Starter
- Fish Food

- Fish Net
- Bucket
- Siphon Vacuum

Step 1 – Where to Place Your Aquarium

Even small aquariums are extremely heavy when full, with just the water weighing about 8.3 pounds per gallon – plus the gravel and the aquarium itself. A fully set up 38-gallon aquarium will weigh more than 355 pounds! Try to settle on a permanent spot prior to set up. If you are using an existing piece of furniture in place of a stand manufactured to hold an aquarium, be sure that it will hold the weight.

Additional care should be given to the placement of tanks larger than about 150 gallons, as the floor underneath may not be suitable to hold such weight.

Keep in mind that aquariums receiving direct sunlight will grow an abundance of algae. While algae are not harmful to fish, it will mean more cleaning to do later. Avoid putting your aquarium near a window.

Step 2 – Leveling Your Aquarium

Whether you have purchased an aquarium stand or are using existing furniture, make sure the base is level before you begin filling your aquarium. Once the aquarium is filled, it will be obvious if the tank is not level. This is not a good step to skip!

Use a level to check front to back, side to side, and from corner to corner. Use shims under the stand at the floor until the tank is level.

When installing the aquarium on carpet, know that wood or metal strips are often used to secure carpet to the floor and to keep it flat. These strips are installed close walls. If the aquarium is placed on a strip, it will raise up the back of the aquarium. If possible, space the aquarium from the wall in front of the strip.

Once shims are placed under the stand and the tank reads as level, you are ready to move on.

Step 3 – Preparing the Aquarium

Using a soft cloth or damp paper towel, wipe down the inside the of the aquarium to remove dirt and dust. Never use soap or household cleaning agents in or on your aquarium.

Step 4 – Adding a Background

The background is attached to the outside back of the aquarium to hide the filter and electrical cords. It adds depth to your tank and can create a pleasing setting.

Clean and dry the back of the aquarium to prepare it for the background. Cut the background to the exact length of the aquarium. Using clear tape, attach the right and left sides to your aquarium. Next, attach the top edge of the background. Run a piece of tape the entire length of the aquarium to keep drips and splashes from getting between the background and the aquarium.

If a solid color is desired – typically blue or black – spray paint can be used to coat the back of the tank before the tank is put in place. Choose the desired color in waterproof or water-resistant matte finish. Only use spray paint outdoors or in a well-ventilated area. Use painters' tape and plastic to protect from unwanted overspray. Spray the tank upside down so that no paint gets into the tank. Allow the paint to dry fully before moving the tank. A razorblade can be used with caution to scrape off painted backgrounds.

In general, dark colored gravel and backgrounds will contrast more with fish to accentuate the colors of community fish and make them pop.

Step 5 – Adding Gravel

If the gravel you chose looks dusty or dirty, rinse it in a large bucket, 10 to 15 pounds at a time. Run clean tap water through it, stirring gently with your hand, and drain the bucket to rinse away dust, debris, and color flakes. A kitchen colander also works very well.

Add enough gravel to create a layer between ½ inch and 1 inch thick for a fish-only aquarium. For most aquariums, this will be a little less than a pound per gallon of tank volume. An aquarium with live plants needs smaller gravel particles and a deeper base of 3 to 4 inches.

In metric units: 1.25-2.5cm of gravel for fish-only; 7.5-10cm for planted aquariums.

Step 6 – Adding Filtration

There are several types of filters that can be used with your aquarium. To choose which filter is right for your tank, see Chapter 1: Equipment to Create a Freshwater Aquarium.

Most tops have cut-outs at the back to accommodate the filter. Glass lids come with plastic back strips that can be trimmed to fit the filter. Position a power filter or tubing for a canister filter to align with the cut-outs or where the back strip will be trimmed. Follow the manufacturer's instructions for setting up the filter appropriately. If the intake tube can be adjusted, the intake should be set to about two-thirds of the way from the top of the aquarium. For optimal flow, the intake and return for a canister filter should be in opposite back corners.

Do not start the filter at this time. Without water the filter pump will be damaged.

Step 7 – Attaching a Heater

Nearly all modern heaters are fully submersible, and most have pre-calibrated thermostats built in. Follow the manufacturer's instructions to calibrate the heater if necessary. Secure the heater to the glass with the included suction cups. The ideal location for the heater is near the filter's return so that the water flow will disperse the warm water throughout the aquarium.

Large tanks may require two heaters on opposite sides of the tank to adequately heat the large volume without creating pockets of warm water and cold water.

Do not plug in the heater at this time. Without water the heater will quickly overheat and be damaged.

Step 8 – Decorating Your Aquarium

Rinse all rocks, artificial plants, and other décor. Smaller, shorter plants should be placed in the front of the aquarium, with larger, taller ones toward the back.

First, if you are using driftwood in your aquarium, place it a little towards the back. The driftwood can be the focal point with decorative rocks and plants as accents. Rocks and driftwood are used to create levels, like caves, in your aquarium for fish to swim through.

Experiment with positioning the décor in different places. Be creative with this enjoyable step! There are many ways to aquascape your aquarium; the most important part is that you are happy with the way it looks. Remember, you can always make changes.

Next, water will be added to the aquarium. Now is a good time to review the previous steps, since making changes will be much more difficult once the tank is full.

Step 9 – Adding Water to Your Aquarium

For smaller aquariums a 5-gallon bucket filled at the kitchen faucet or bath tub is all you will need to fill the tank. Try to adjust the water temperature to between 80°F and 82°F (~27°C) directly at the faucet.

For larger aquariums, carrying water back and forth may take too much time and energy; unless you're looking for a workout, you may want to use a garden hose. If you do, let water run through the hose for several minutes before filling your aquarium to flush stagnant water from the hose.

When using a garden hose, you can adjust the temperature by adding hot water, but only after the tank is partially full. Hot water directly on cold glass can cause the glass to crack.

There are some useful maintenance kits available which you can use to fill your aquarium and that attach directly to a kitchen faucet with 25 to 50 feet of tubing. These kits can also be used to vacuum the aquarium directly into the sink.

Whatever method you use to fill your aquarium, it is important to avoid stirring up the gravel while pouring in the water. You just took time to arrange your decorations. Dumping water carelessly onto the gravel will mess up your work! It may also cause a cloudy tank, especially if the gravel was not sufficiently rinsed. Pour the water (or point the hose) onto a large rock or decoration. You can also place a dinner plate in the tank temporarily and pour water over that.

Fill the tank to over the bottom of the top frame, or about ¾ of an inch below the top of the aquarium.

Step 10 – Install a Thermometer

Attach a hanging thermometer to the aquarium on the side opposite the heater, about three inches from the top of the aquarium. Keeping a thermometer in the aquarium allows you to confirm that the heater is working properly and that in hot summer months the aquarium is not too warm.

Step 11 – Start the Filter

Now it's time to prime the filter. Using a cup or pitcher, begin filling the filter manually before plugging it in. If the filter doesn't start running, continue filling it manually until the pump fully engages. If your filter uses cartridges or carbon, rinse them before use.

Your filter should turn over the water in the aquarium between 5 to 8 times per hour.

Step 12 – Plug in the Heater

Allow the heater to adjust to the temperature of the aquarium before plugging it in to prevent the glass from cracking. The heater should be set between 80°F to 82°F (~27°C) for the first four to six weeks until the biological filter is established. Once your aquarium is cycled (see Chapter 3: Water Quality), set the temperature to 74-76°F (~24°C).

Step 13 – Topping Your Aquarium

Remove the tabs or trim the plastic back strip to fit the location of your filter. Place the hood or glass tops on the aquarium and plug in your light.

For planted aquariums, the light should be on between 10 to 12 hours per day. With no live plants, run the light for no more than 8 hours per day. When the photoperiod is too long, your aquarium water may eventually turn an unsightly green or red from algae.

Standard light fixtures that come with most starter kits are not suitable for growing plants. Low-light plants like java fern may do well enough, but most require a more powerful light to thrive. If you have a standard fixture, artificial plants are best.

Step 14 – The Final Step: Water Conditioner

Add a good water conditioner to neutralize harmful chlorine and chloramines. Follow the manufacturer's instructions for the dosage. Even freshwater fish require a small amount of salt, which should be added at this time unless you have live plants.

Fish

After all this knowledge you have gained on choosing the right equipment and setting up your tank properly, let us finally get to the centerpiece of your home aquarium: Your new best friends! We will cover how to pick out healthy fish, how many you should purchase, and compatibility. Then we will move on to beginner-friendly aquarium inhabitants!

Buying Healthy Fish

There are several things you should look for when you go to pick out your new fin friends. The first thing you are likely to notice is their activity level. While some species are more active than others, there aren't many that are happy to just float around placidly, especially at the very top or bottom of the tank. Most fish are inquisitive creatures. Some are even territorial, so more often than not, you will see them exploring their surroundings, interacting with other fish, and searching for food. If you have doubts about potential fish's activity level at a store, ask to see them being fed. Even the most inactive species will perk up when it is dinner time!

The next thing to consider is coloration. Have a good idea of what the species you are interested in looks like before you get to the store. This way, if the fish for sale look dull, their fins are unhealthy, or they have any suspicious spots or discoloration, you will know that you should look elsewhere. I love doing this ahead of time, so I can plan out what kind of color schemes and activity levels I want. It is a great activity to do while your tank is cycling to pass the time!

Sometimes fish will show no outward signs of illness or disease. Even if they are showing symptoms, it can often be difficult for us humans to spot. Some common signs of illness are: protruding eyes, gasping for breath, very light or very dark spots, abnormal swimming patterns, overproduction of mucus, and fungal growth (it looks like your fish swam through thick cobwebs). Keeping an eye out for these signs will help you get the healthiest fish possible.

Fish Quantity

A common problem for first time aquarists (and sometimes experienced ones too!) is overstocking. Overstocking means that you have too many fish and not enough space for them to feel comfortable. As mentioned in Chapter 1, a good rule of thumb is to have no more than one inch of fish for every gallon of water your aquarium can hold. However, this is dependent on what kind of fish you keep and how much actual space is in your tank. If you plan to have a thick layer of substrate and a jungle-like overgrowth of plants, you may need to subtract a few to several gallons from your 1-gallon/1-inch estimate.

Another thing to ponder when considering a fish purchase is if the species you would like are schooling or shoaling fish. These types of fish will only be their happiest if they are in groups of their own kind. Whether in a store or online, any respectable fish seller will have suggestions on how many individuals of each species should be kept together. A general tip is to keep shoaling and schooling fish in groups of at least 6-10.

Fish Compatibility

Freshwater aquarium fish are usually classified as either peaceful, semi-aggressive, and aggressive. Peaceful fish are great for a community tank. They get along great with almost all other peaceful community fish. They generally will not bother or harass snails, frogs, and other fish. If peaceful fish are large enough, they may occasionally eat small aquarium shrimp or their newly hatched babies, but adult shrimp are usually too big to be considered a snack for peaceful fish. I highly recommend beginning aquarists start with a peaceful community tank. They are generally the easiest to care for, and you will not have to worry about them injuring or killing each other. Examples of peaceful fish are danios, rasboras, guppies, and mollies.

Semi-aggressive aquarium fish are usually able to be housed with their own species or other semi-aggressive fish if there are enough of them to spread the aggression around. This way, a pecking order is established where each fish knows its place in the social hierarchy, and no individual is singled out to get picked on relentlessly. Examples of semi-aggressive fish are freshwater angelfish, gouramis, and loaches.

Aggressive fish are those that will defend their territory against all other fish, even their own kind. I recommend beginners steer clear from aggressive fish unless you can keep a single individual by itself in a tank, such as a betta fish. Aggressive species generally need a high protein diet, as they are usually predators in the wild. Live, frozen, and freeze-dried meaty foods should be a staple of their diet. Examples of aggressive species are dwarf pea puffers, tiger barbs, and many species of cichlids.

Great Beginner Fish

In general, it is better to start as an aquarist with smaller or medium-sized fish. Different fish do require different types of treatment, and it would be a shame to accidentally kill some of these beautiful creatures. So, I really recommend starting off small and simple. Enjoy your little friends and as you gain more knowledge and confidence, level up slowly to more challenging species. Remember, just because they are smaller or easier to care for does not make them any less beautiful and interesting! Here is my list of great fish and other aquarium animals that are quite beginner-friendly. Find out which ones are right for you! Many aquarists like to have activity at different levels of their tank, so the following list is arranged by preferred swim levels.

Top Swimmers

Danios

Danios are some of my all-time favorite fish for all aquarists, beginner or not! They are super active little fish that are a ton of fun to watch — it is like they are almost always playing! Most varieties only grow to about two inches in length. A social fish, they like to be in groups of at least five or six. Some of the most popular danio varieties are named after the way they look, like zebra danios, leopard fin danios, and glofish (which glow under blacklight!). They get along well in almost any community tank, but their active lifestyle can be intimidating to some shyer fish. If you have any shyer fish, make sure to pay attention during feeding time so that no group of fish outcompetes others for food.

Bettas

While bettas can be found at all levels of the tank, they are put on the top swimmer's list because of their unique anatomy. They have special organs that allow them to breathe air, so access to the top of your tank is a must for them. They are stunning fish that come in tons of colors and several types of fin styles. They like to eat specialized betta pellets and small meaty foods like freeze-dried bloodworms.

Beginners should keep the more decorative male bettas on their own, though. They are very territorial, and even female bettas are known to fight each other if not kept under precise parameters. Once you have more aquarium experience under your belt, there are some other species that can be kept with bettas. Still, it's best for beginners to just have one betta in a tank on their own, with maybe a nerite snail or two to clean up uneaten food. Like goldfish, bettas are commonly seen in tiny bowls, but to keep them alive, happy, and healthy, they will need at least a five-gallon tank with a proper filter, heater, and pump. Under these conditions, they usually live from three to five years.

Middle Swimmers

Goldfish

Goldfish are probably one of the most recognizable fish in the world. They are also commonly misunderstood. Because they gained notoriety by being kept in bowls and given away as carnival prizes, it is assumed that they can live comfortably in small spaces. Nothing could be further from the truth! Goldfish actually grow up to a foot long in the wild and often reach up to ten inches in a home aquarium, so they need plenty of space. It is fine if they have smaller tanks when they are first bought, but they will need to be transferred to a bigger space as they grow.

Despite being common, they are still absolutely stunning fish. Their peaceful nature and gentle movements are sure to make you feel relaxed! They come in all kinds of colors and body shapes and are easy to feed. They will eat almost any commercially available fish flakes. They do produce a lot of waste, but if you keep up with regular tank maintenance, they are a breeze to care for!

Platies and Mollies

Platies and mollies are excellent choices for your first aquarium! They are incredibly hardy little fish that come in cool colors like red, orange, black, and my favorite, black and white spotted. They can adapt to almost any normal water parameters, so they are very forgiving fish if you make a few mistakes along the way. They are generally active swimmers and will readily accept most kinds of flaked food.

Guppies and Endler's Live Bearers

Guppies are one of the most popular freshwater species due to their vast array of colors, lively personalities, and how easy it is to breed them. Endler's livebearers come from the same family as guppies, but their bodies are usually the colorful part, and they have smaller tails. Guppies often have the most color on their long, flowy tails. Both are very easy to care for and will readily eat almost any kind of commercially available fish flakes.

Bottom Swimmers

Corydoras

Corydoras, also known as Corys or Cory Cats, are fun little mini catfish that are just so cute! They are active, curious bottom-dwellers that are always on the lookout for food. They come in various colors and stay very small, measuring in full-grown at only 1-2.5 inches. While it is possible to keep a single Cory, they are happiest in groups of 3 or more. Super adaptable and easy to care for, they are an excellent choice for a beginner community tank.

Bristlenose Plecos

While larger species of plecos will grow quite large, the Bristlenose Plecos stays at a much more manageable 3-5 inches when fully grown – which is perfect for medium-sized beginner tanks. They come in colors that range from albino white to jet black with white spots, but they are mostly found in a greenish-grey hue.

Beginner to Intermediate Fish

Angelfish

Freshwater angelfish are beautiful fish that come in a variety of colors and patterns. While they are somewhat adaptable to water parameters, they need a big tank, 50+ gallons to be at their best. Because they grow to around 8 inches in height and six inches in length, they need a large, tall aquarium with lots of vertically growing plants to be their happiest. They like to have others of their own kind to socialize with but can be territorial.

Loaches

Loaches are great if you are looking for cute fish that like to hang out at the bottom of the tank. My favorites are the yo-yo loach, a black and white fish whose stripes seem to spell out 'yoyo' when they are young, and skunk loaches, who have tan bodies with a black stripe running down their spine. Different species of loaches have different personalities. In my experience, yo-yos are quite active, swimming up to the top of the tank when they know it is feeding time and eagerly exploring their environment during the day. Skunks seem to be shyer, being more active at night and preferring to take shelter in rock caves and dense vegetation. I would classify these fish as beginner to intermediate friendly, as like the angelfish, they like to have others of their kind around, but can be territorial and shy around other aggressive or semi-aggressive fish.

African Dwarf Frogs

African dwarf frogs are one of the only fully aquatic frog species. They are super fun to watch, and 2-3 frogs can be kept in as small as a 5-gallon tank. They are positively adorable little frogs that only grow to about 2 inches. However, I would classify these as perfect for beginner to intermediate aquarists. They are sensitive to water parameters and need to have easy access to the surface as they still need access to the top of the tank to get extra oxygen.

Clean-up Crew

Cherry and Ghost Shrimp

These little shrimps are remarkable to have as a clean-up crew and are tons of fun to watch. They constantly graze at the bottom of the tank to scavenge for uneaten food, algae, and decaying plant matter. Although they are scavengers, you should not count on there being enough leftovers and dead plants to keep them happy. Sinking algae pellets should be their primary source of food, with scavenging for scraps as a supplement.

In addition to helping keep your tank clean, their grazing and swimming bring activity to the bottom of your tank. As the name implies, cherry shrimp are a lovely bright red color, whereas ghost shrimp are entirely transparent! It is fascinating to watch them eat as you can see their internal organs. They both can be a little shy, so be sure to have some plant cover or caves for them to hide in. Having bolt-holes when they feel threatened will give them the courage to come out and play more often and display their best colors. You can keep them with any peaceful community fish and even semi-aggressive species if the fish are too small to consider a one-inch shrimp to be a tasty snack.

Snails

While you may be skeptical, some freshwater snails are super interesting to watch! Mystery snails come in tons of different colors and show far more activity than you would expect from a snail. They generally have solid colors like white, black, gold, purple, green, and more! Their shells are usually solid or banded, and their bodies are a lighter version of their shell color with iridescent spots. One prominent feature of the mystery snail is their long antennas, which are constantly in motion, searching for food and danger. You might also notice a tube-like structure, about half the length of their antennae, which is used to siphon water to their gills.

They are small enough (two to three inches) that you can keep one to two of them in as small as a five-gallon tank, but interesting enough to be at home in even the largest community tanks. They are completely peaceful and, like the shrimps above, are remarkable as a cleanup crew. But also, like shrimp, leftovers and dead leaves will only satisfy them between regular feedings of plant-based, sinking pellets. Happy, healthy mystery snails love to go right up to the top of the tank (secured lid necessary!), then curl up and float down to the bottom – Whee!

Nerite snails are another excellent option for a beginner cleanup crew that is low profile. They usually have a base color that is olive green, light to dark brown, or a dark gold, so they blend in with many naturally scaped tanks. One of the most interesting features of the nerite snail is their shell pattern. They often have whorls, zebra stripes, and dots. No two shells are the same! The only downside to the nerite is that they can lay off-white eggs all over your tank. Still, they rarely hatch, almost never survive, and are relatively easy to remove. The social and behavioral nature of nerites is much like the mystery snail, although they are slower moving.

Special Note on Snails

You should be careful about what kind of snails you introduce to your tank. Many snails can reproduce asexually, which means a single snail can produce thousands of babies if they only have enough food, space, and time. Pond snails are generally considered a nuisance and will reproduce rapidly. They do not cause much harm in small numbers, but they can overrun a tank with minimal effort and destroy plants, which can set off a chain reaction that can ruin your whole ecosystem.

Assassin snails are great for eating pond snails but can also become problematic in themselves. While both can be beneficial to your aquarium, for beginners, it is best to avoid them and remove them from your tank immediately if you notice them. You should take preventative measures before adding anything to your tank. But nerite and mystery snails generally do not reproduce to a nuisance level with proper tank maintenance.

These colorful jewels will be the highlight of your home decoration, but how can you ensure the health and safety of your new pets? Now that you know what to look for in your new best friends, how to pick out healthy fish, how many you should acquire, and what kind of fish will get along together, we will move on to aquarium fish care. So, how do you take care of them so they can live their best life? In the next chapter, you will learn what to feed your fish, how much and how often to feed them, Common diseases (and how to treat them), and common mistakes that will put your fish in danger of dying.

How to Properly Set Up Your Aquarium

Tank Size Does Matter

Before setting up your own Freshwater Aquarium, keep in mind that tank size does matter and it is crucial. It is the basic element that will affect your time, effort, materials, and budget. Tank size and shape will vary depending on your personal taste and choice.

However, you may want consider the following factors to help you organize your thoughts.

Determine the area or space in your home where you would like to place the aquarium. Think of a size that would complement the aesthetic design of that space.

When carefully planned, an aquarium can add a magical transformation to your home's aesthetic values. Be sure to pick a spot that is out of the direct sunlight; since sunlight can affect the water temperature and increase the growth of algae.

Think of the number of fishes and kind of species that you want to keep. Obviously, the more or larger the species are, the wider the tank should also be.

Typically, you may follow the ratio of 1 inch of fish is to 1 gallon of water. There are fishes that grow in only an inch or two.

If you choose that kind of species and decide to keep just a few inhabitants, a standard size (20-40 gallon fish tank) will be enough.

It is important to know that smaller tanks are not recommended for novice hobbyists. Changes in water chemistry can bring harmful effects that are difficult to minimize in smaller tanks.

If you want to house more fishes and choose tropical species that grow more in length, you may opt for a larger tank. There is no limit in choosing a tank size.

There are even aquariums that measure as large as 180-gallon (72" x 24" x 25"). However, keep in mind that the maintenance of larger tanks may also become overwhelming in the long run.

Choosing a Substrate

Consider the kind of substrate that you want to use. Substrate refers to the material mantled at the bottom of the tank.

The substrate can have an impact on filtration, water chemistry, and the inhabitants' health. More so, it can extensively affect the tank's aesthetics.

There are several choices of substrates such as sand, pebbles, neon-colored gravel, marbles, and corals. Among these, gravel is the most common.

It comes in different sizes and colors which are mostly vivid; adding more life to the aquarium. Gravel also contains a nutrient called laterite which may be beneficial to the plant's growth.

However, there are species that do not suit a gravel bottom. If you want to keep a Corydoras catfish, for example, a gravel bottom must be crossed out of your options.

This species tend to hunt underneath in search of food; something that would be difficult to do in a sea of gravel. More so, sharp gravel may damage their barbels.

Even the popular home aquarium star, gold fish, may be put in danger as it can swallow pieces of gravel. Although the gravel can still be removed from the throat, doing so might still put the gold fish in a lot stress.

Sand may not be as popular as gravel but it provides easy maintenance when used correctly. Dirt particles would not sift through underneath but would just rather stay on top.

Just like gravel, sand also contains laterite that provides benefits for live plants. When using sand, opt for the coarser and medium grains.

Fine grains of sand hinder root development of live plants and have higher chances of becoming anaerobic. Also, be careful in planting live plants through the sand as the laterite may blur the water.

Big rocks and marbles can also be used as substrates as they have good decorative effects. However, it would be better if rocks remain as embellishments instead.

Bacteria can easily grow on them and there are times when fishes get stuck between these rocks.

Aragonite and corals may look attractive when used as substrates. However, these materials are not recommended as they lower the water's pH level.

Unless you are thinking of maintaining a brackish aquarium, a low pH level is something to avoid. Corals can easily attract dirt; affecting the water quality.

Between corals and aragonite, the latter is much recommended by aquarists but its downside would be its very expensive price.

Going for a bare bottom, on the other hand, requires more analysis as it is not suitable to every kind of inhabitants. Freshwater tanks are good enough for bare bottoms but saltwater tanks are not.

In terms of plant decors, tanks that contain corals can survive in naked bottoms but real plants obviously can't. However, if you only want to keep the famous gold fish, going bare-bottom may be suitable for easier cleaning.

Since gold fish is one untidy species, it requires constant cleaning. Therefore, a bare bottom may become an advantage.

Live Plants Vs Fake Plants

We rarely see a freshwater aquarium that does not come with a plant decor. Due to the fresh look it provides, plant is the top choice for fish tank embellishments.

It makes an aquarium more alive as it mimics the genuine feel of nature. It also provides hiding spots for the fishes; making them feel secure.

Most fish owners prefer plastic plants for their aquariums. First of all, artificial plants provide easy maintenance as their leaves do not fall and wither.

Just like live plants, they also give the inhabitants a space for hiding. Artificial plants are made to appear more vivid than live ones.

However, the most common artificial plants are made of a lightweight bottom. As time goes by, it becomes a pain in the eye as it would usually float in the water.

There are some fake plants, though, that are made of heavy bottoms. However, they would cost much than the lightweight ones. Since artificially colored plants are designed to look more vibrant, the cheaper varieties can look unnatural.

Live plants may not be as vibrant as the fake ones. However, they provide benefits that artificial plants cannot duplicate.

Live plants improve the quality of water and provide a balanced ecosystem for the inhabitants. Obviously, they can provide a natural habitat for the fishes. They provide substantial levels of oxygen that help the fishes breathe.

They help the pH level rest on its normal range. However, when real plants die, they cause a spike in the tank's nitrogen level.

This eventually stresses the fishes. Uncontrolled and high levels of nitrogen will become lethal. Therefore, live plants require more maintenance and constant observation than fake ones.

In terms of cost, real plants are more expensive than artificial plants.

Fishes would not really care if the plants around them are live or fake. They would not even be able to tell the difference.

Plants, whether real or artificial, provide the same function to the inhabitants —realistic environment and shelter.

Choosing the Decors

Fish tank adornments can make your aquarium stand-out. They are like accessories to a boring outfit; they can add instant magic to the tank's over-all aesthetic.

They can set the mood and theme. More so, they also provide safety and comfort to the inhabitants.

In choosing your decors, keep a theme that you want to carry out and stick with it. Example, if you want a nature-themed aquarium that resembles real aquatic habitat, adorn the tank with decors akin to what can be seen in nature.

These may include live plants to provide greenery and rock formations to mimic the ocean.

You may also adorn the tank based on your personality. Example, if you have a fun personality, you may add blasts of colors in the aquarium; such as colored plants or multi-colored rocks.

Complement them with the inhabitants by choosing rainbowfish or clown fish. You may also decorate the tank based on its constant viewers.

Example, if you have a little girl in the house who serves as the fishes' constant audience, entertain her by creating a fairytale-themed aquarium. Put a castle with holes where fishes can swim through.

If you do not want to put a castle, you may simply put a castle background. Add fairy objects or mermaid accessories.

While it may be tempting to gather possible decors and accessories in and out of the house (the beach, for example), be careful in doing so; as these accessories may contain parasites that can harm the inhabitants.

More so, avoid decorating the tank with copper and painted objects. These contain poisonous chemicals. Avoid objects with sharp edges as well.

Lighting the Tank

Just like any other community, lighting is also essential in an aquatic habitat. Aside from good quality water, good lighting boosts the plants' natural growth.

Scientifically, light is crucial as plants undergo photosynthesis to live and remain healthy. Generally, plants will do fine in a moderate light.

However, there are plants that require more intense lighting than other species; such as plants with a touch of red in the stem or leaves.

Light also affects the fishes' health and enrich their colors. More so, good lighting allows you to closely observe the activities in the tank; making it easier to prevent if there are any arising problems.

Now that you have probably thought on the kind of fishes and plants that you want, choosing the type of light to be used will be based on these factors.

The most traditional lighting used by aquarists is the tubular Standard Fluorescent Light. First off, this type is a lot cheaper and easily available.

Despite the cheap price, it can provide good lighting to support plant growth. There are also several choices of a fluorescent light.

There are types that are warmer, types that give off white and blue light mimicking marine habitat, types that give deep blue shade mimicking deep underwater, and types that are called plant bulbs which is beneficial for photosynthesis.

You may easily purchase one that complements the theme you have chosen. However, this type of light does not lasts long compared to others; so you may need to replace it often. Also, it emits more heat and does not provide a gleam similar to that of the ocean water.

Another type of lighting is the Compact Florescent Light. Unlike the standard one that comes in a single tube, the compact type combines two or more tube bulbs for better lighting. It has the same advantages that come in a standard fluorescent – cheaper, easily available, easy to operate, and has a wide selection of colors.

However, a single compact lighting fixture can do the job of a two individual tube fluorescent. Therefore, a compact type is more space-saving. Metal Halide is also an option for freshwater aquariums because it mimics natural sunlight.

It is especially recommended for very large tanks; something deeper than 24 inches. It consists of halide salt and mercury vapor.

Physically, it has a main bulb that is connected to another arc bulb through wires. The vapor and salt produces light as electricity passes through the arc bulb.

It gives a shimmering effect to the water as the light deeply passes through the tank. It does not require constant replacement because it is long-lasting. However, this type may be quite expensive.

In this modern era of fishkeeping, an innovative type of lighting has been recently introduced. Most modern tanks already use a LED (Light Emitting Diode).

This newcomer can benefit both real and artificial plants as it provides a pure and deeply penetrating light. It comes in varying colors that mimic a natural freshwater hue or complement the fishes and plants' natural glow.

It is also more energy-saving and does not give off too much heat. Just like a metal halide, it provides shimmer on the water similar to an ocean's shiny glow. However, an LED is also expensive.

Other Aquarium Products and Accessories

Aside from the aesthetics, keeping an aquarium must also involve mechanical and scientific equipment to ensure that everything is working properly.

A heater ensures that the tank's temperature remains stable. Fish do not produce their own body heat unlike human and other mammals.

Therefore, it is important to maintain a stable tank temperature because the fishes rely on it to maintain their own body heat. There are two types of heater, the submersible and external.

Do not use a heater that is too large for your tank as it may cause heating problems.

A thermometer works hand in hand with the heater. Changes in the water temperature may cause possible problems to the tank.

Unfortunately, these changes cannot be observed just by watching over the tank. You need a thermometer to track the temperature.

There are different types of thermometer. Standing or floating thermometers allow you to directly measure the water temperature by placing it inside the aquarium.

There are thermometer types that simply float in the water, weighted types that sink at the bottom of the water, one that uses a suction cup, and a hanging type.

These are inexpensive types and not affected by room temperature. However, these types may be difficult to read as the scale is much smaller than the others.

Also, these are made of glass so they can possibly be broken especially if you have larger fishes. Another type of thermometer is the digital thermometer.

It comes with a reader that is placed inside the tank. The temperature it reads will be reflected on the small screen device that is placed outside.

There are very modern models that come with an alert tone that alarms when the temperature goes above or below the expected level. This type can be very efficient as it can provide the most accurate reading.

However, it is the most expensive type. A LCD or Stick-on Thermometer is also available.

This type is the most commonly used as it is inexpensive, versatile, easy to use and can be easily placed in any location. However, it can be less accurate than the digital type and can be hard to read in low-light.

A filtration system or simply filter is another important accessory in setting up a freshwater aquarium. It removes harmful chemicals, fish manure, floating particles, left over feeds, decaying organic materials and other toxins from the water.

When left unremoved, these toxins can cause ammonia spike which can cause death to the fishes. You might say that you can always conduct a cleaning routine every day.

However, deep-cleaning can actually cause shock and stress to the fishes. A filter helps in cleaning the tank without the stressful process.

There are basically three types of filtration: Chemical, Mechanical, and Biological. Through a mechanical filtration, the water is pushed to a medium that acts as a strainer.

The strainer can come in a form of pads, filter floss, or a sponge. It sips the free-floating particles present in the water without interrupting the water chemistry.

It comes in different types and sizes. Extra fine mechanical medium can remove extra small particles including bacteria and parasites. A coarse to medium grade type can remove the most visible debris.

A very coarse medium grade type absorbs extra-large debris. The larger the medium is, the larger the particles that it can extract. The larger medium can also be easier to clean than a fine one.

A biological filter helps in breaking down bacteria and other microorganisms. In turn, these bacteria and microorganisms will be converted into less harmful by-products.

A biological filter also comes in different types. A smaller one can last for 2-4 years and is the best option if you have a smaller tank.

It may be small in size but it is reliable enough in absorbing a lot of bacteria. A plastic biological filter, on the other hand, may not have a wide surface area. However, it does not clog easily and can even survive longer than the other types.

A chemical filter removes toxins from the water through chemical resins and activated carbons. This type of filter is not commonly used compared to a mechanical and biological one.

However, it can also be a good accessory in maintaining good water quality as it removes unwanted particles and matter that adheres to it.

Types of Water

In setting up a freshwater aquarium, it is common for hobbyists to use tap water because of its easier availability. Tap water is cleansed using several chemicals to kill the bacteria and make it safe for human consumption.

However, these chemicals, such as chlorine and chloramine, can harm the fishes. If using tap water, you must check first its nitrate level, gH, kH and pH level.

You must also clean the water using a chloramine remover or dechlorinator.

Tap water may work fine but it can still be disadvantageous to the fishes. The best option you have in lieu of the tap water is spring water.

When choosing a brand of spring water, make sure that it is not distilled as it means that the water has already been stripped off of minerals.

To ensure that the water is free from harmful substances, such as mercury, copper or zinc, and that it is detoxified, you may use a water conditioner. It neutralizes chlorine and other unwanted materials in the water.

It is a bottled solution that is added in the water, especially if you really have no choice but to use tap water. A typical water conditioner is recommended to be used in a ratio of 2 teaspoons per 10 gallons of water.

Setting up the tank

After a thorough planning on the materials, theme, size, and accessories that you want for your freshwater aquarium, it is now time to set it up.

Clean the tank first using a clean soft sponge and warm water to erase extra residue and get rid of harmful chemicals in the tank, if there are any. Do not use any kind of soap in cleaning the tank as it may leave residues that may harm the fishes.

Next, set up the tank in a steady base. The tank itself may be carried easily but once it is filled with water, it becomes heavy. So, be sure to place it in a stable base that is strong enough to hold the aquarium's weight.

If you are placing the aquarium beside the wall, make a 5' allowance to make enough room for the filter.

Fill in the tank with the gravel or your chosen substrate; then, add the other decorations. Ensure of the cleanliness of the materials that must be submerged inside the aquarium.

In cleaning the decors, you may simply wash them off over running water. Other embellishments like driftwood, rocks, or shells may need extra scrubbing to get rid of parasites and dirt.

In cleaning the substrate like gravel, simply submerge it in a bucket of water to remove dirt; then, strain to remove other unwanted particles.

By this time, the live plants may be added in the aquarium. Be sure to wash them first under running water to get rid of unwanted parasites and deposits.

Check if there are decaying roots and leaves on the plants. Begin placing the taller plants at the back area followed by the smaller ones at the front. Ideally, these plants will hide the other equipment.

Arrange the wood or rock decorations as desired. Then, put a base fertilizer if you are using live plants. Add in the substrate; make a sloping direction towards the back of the tank.

Set up the other equipment. Assemble and install the filter behind the tank.

Install the thermometer in your desired position or in a spot that would allow easier monitoring. Set up the heater and wait for about 15 minutes or until its thermostat has adapted to the water temperature.

Install the light and hood in the aquarium. Be sure that the power cords will not get wet. After that, turn the equipment on to see if everything is working properly.

Next, add in the spring water. To avoid disarranging the substrate and other decors, place a saucer or plate on top of the gravel.

Then, pour the water directly onto the plate. If you have no choice but to add tap water, make sure to use a water conditioner.

Leave the set-up for a day or so until the nitrogen cycle has completed before adding the fish. Once the temperature has stabilized, turn off the electric equipment.

Then, add the first fish (or two). Wait for another six weeks or until the nitrite and ammonia levels have dropped to zero before adding all the other additional fishes.

Lighting For Your Aquarium

Before, aquarium lighting was a frequently neglected part of aquarium keeping. Be that as it may, we now realize that normal lighting assumes an indispensable part in the accomplishment of all aquarium systems. The nature of aquatic life in your aquarium can be straightforwardly identified with the nature of light. On the off chance that the right range and power of light are not well given, the survival rate of the corals, plants, or fish will be sick. At the point when planning your aquarium lighting framework, your objective ought to be to copy standard conditions. On account of slow progressions in lighting innovation, this has turned into a less demanding errand.

All lighting frameworks produce heat. The all the more capable the lighting context, the more noteworthy the cooling prerequisites are prone to be. Despite the size or kind of your lighting frame, your aquarium ought to be situated in a temperature-controlled space to offset the deep heat.

In its most fundamental part, aquarium lighting permits specialists to watch aquarium occupants. Be that as it may, all the more critically, normal aquarium lighting gives essential vitality to photosynthetic plants and creatures. As the essential light source (and by and large, the primary light source), appropriate aquarium lighting is vital for any framework that contains photosynthetic living beings, for example, plants, anemones, or corals. Lighting likewise impacts fish conduct and physiology and is indispensable for the general wellbeing and prosperity of the whole aquarium.

Diverse Light Bulbs and Light Fixtures for Different Setups

There are wide assortments of lighting choices for aquarists. This different choice permits specialists of all levels to give the right lighting conditions to their specific aquarium tenants. Aquarium light apparatuses are by and largely assembled into four general classifications (from most established innovation to most creative): Normal yield fluorescent lighting, minimal fluorescent lighting, and high force (intensity) metal halide lighting and LED (Light Emitting Diode) frameworks.

Typical Output Fluorescent Lighting

Additionally called Standard Fluorescent Lights, these flexible lighting structures are the least demanding approach to lighting an aquarium. They are the easiest. Bright light (Fluorescent) apparatuses are an awesome decision for new and saltwater fish-just aquariums. The vast choice of knobs or bulbs accessible for these simple to-utilize, reasonable, and energy efficient light apparatuses permits the specialist to customize aquarium lighting. Use diverse globules (bulbs) to give the right light to your aquarium occupants.

Minimized Fluorescents

Minimized fluorescent are higher light yield forms of standard glaring light frameworks. Rather than single tube globules (bulbs), smaller fluorescent frames join double or quad tube bulbs for more great light yield from a solitary bulb. A solitary minimal glaring light apparatus effectively does the occupation of two standard fluorescent installations. This space-sparing component makes conservative fluorescent frameworks a great decision when updating from standard fluorescent frames. Luckily, reduced bright light frameworks are not any harder to work and keep up than standard glaring light frameworks. These independent lighting frames are anything but difficult to work, and since they are a kind of open light framework, it has every one of the advantages of fluorescent lighting. For instance, low working cost, less warmth outflow, and a wide choice of bulbs with little heat emission are perfect for both freshwater and marine applications.

Metals Halides

Metal halides frameworks are high-intensity release (HID) lighting frameworks mainstream are popular among numerous advanced aquarium specialists. Metal halide globules (bulbs) are including a primary glass bulb with a progression of wires connecting another glass bulb (circular segment tube) inside of it. At the point when the power goes through the bend tube, the gasses and metal salts contained inside of the tube deliver light. Not at all like another high-pressure release lighting frameworks (e.g., sodium or mercury vapour lights), the light range and the shading version delivered by metal halides are suited for aquarium use. Metal halide installations are perfect for aquariums, for example, reef aquariums, with inhabitants that require high lighting conditions. Metal halide frameworks are additionally utilized for extensive aquariums or aquariums that are more profound than 24 inches where other lighting frameworks may not be sufficiently adequate to give satisfactory illumination.

Led (Light Emitting Diode)

As a relative "newcomer" to the universe of aquarium lighting, LED light installations are frequently subject to disarray and confusions. Driven innovation utilizes a drastically distinctive way to deal with lighting era. LEDs radiate light as stimulated or emit subatomic particles go through a semiconductor material. This straightforward procedure of light generation called electroluminescence requires little energy to create splendid light for an energy-productive decision to aquarium lighting.

50/50 Actinic White Bulbs - Emit a mix of white and blue light that reproduces marine light conditions. By and large, it is a combination of 10,000°K white light and actinic blue light. This mixed light supports photosynthetic coral development while giving light that is satisfying to the human eye.

Colour (Shading) Enhancing Bulbs - Emit light from the "hotter" end of the shading range to enlarge or improve shading. It is intended to show the shades of your fish to their fullest. It is perfect for fish-only fresh and saltwater aquariums.

Full Spectrum/Daylight Bulbs - Emit every one of the wavelengths of clear light and nearly approximates the visual impacts of normal daylight. It contains a mix of the considerable number of shades of the shading range. These universally good bulbs are perfect for a broad range of fresh and saltwater aquariums.

Actinic Bulbs - Emit light overwhelmingly from the blue end of the shading range. It reproduces light conditions found in deep water and gives the light energy essential to normal photosynthetic coral development. Actinic bulbs are perfect for reef aquariums.

Plant Bulbs - Emit light that invigorates plant development. With light crest emanations in both the red and blue areas of the shading range, this light amplifies photosynthetic action for lavishly planted aquariums.

High-Intensity Bulbs - Emit splendid light with a high shading temperature (Kelvin-rating) running from 10,000°K to 20,000°K. It is a fresh white light ordinarily utilized as a part in conjunction with actinic knobs in marine aquariums. 20,000°K bulbs will transmit a splendid white-blue light that shows up "cooler" to recreate more great marine light conditions

Picking Heating System for Your Aquarium

If you decide to put tropical fish in your aquarium, then you have to ensure the water has the appropriate measure of warmth. To accomplish the water temperature that emulates the warmth of the oceans, the water conditions ought to be in perfect conditions between 20 to 30°C.

The best specialists would let you know, is 24°C. Shockingly, you can't accomplish that by depending on your home's warming framework by any means. What does that mean? You require a different heat radiator for the aquarium. You have to keep the water warm and hold it at that level however much as could reasonably be expected. That is it, plain and straightforward.

What happens if you can't keep a stable tropical temperature in the tank? All things considered, for the especially fragile marine, it could result in stress. What's more, you truly don't need tension in the aquaria. So to dodge that and any of alternate issues that accompany a flimsy warmed aquarium, then below are tips to help you in picking the right heat for the tank.

Size

Here's the principal thing you have to know: aquarium heaters are appraised or rated using watts. In case, you're not certain what heater works for your tank, and then check the packing. Producers have effectively made things simple for you by demonstrating what size of tank the specific heater is useful for.

A certain guideline is that you require 5 watts to warm a gallon of water. Note likewise that the bigger the tank, the slower it loses the warmth. So it's splendidly beautiful to get two heaters for one large tank and split the wattage.

The distinctive sorts of Heaters

Numerous aquarium proprietors utilize an indoor thermostat unit and standard heater. It usually appears as long and thin glass tubes with the warmer at the base and the indoor regulator at the top. It's made to be submerged in the water. It's likewise less expensive, precise and rather advantageous.

There are a ton of other distinctive warmers to look over, as well.

Separate indoor regulator (thermostat): in case you're as of now utilizing an under tank heater, then you simply need to get a different indoor regulator for the tank. This makes things a tad bit less demanding to modify. However, it's a more costly setup.

Under tank warmer mat: very well known back in the 1990's, the aquarium is put on the radiator mat which warms the tank through the glass. A different indoor regulator controls the temperature. It must be expressed that glass isn't the best conductor of warmth, however. Furthermore, the rock at the tank's base won't help in its course, either. If you need to guarantee consistency of warmth; this may not be the best choice.

Heating link (cable): ordinarily added to offer aquarium some assistance with plant development

In-line heater: these sorts of warmers are plumbed into the tubing that is situated between the outside filter and the tank. The water will go through the heater and will be warmed up. The decent thing about in-line warmers is they're produced using plastic that is heat-proof, making them safe to handle. You can likewise make certain they won't be creating any flames. Maybe thus, and the way that they're genuinely new, these warmers are more costly than other different units.

External Heater/filter: likewise called a thermal filter. It's fundamentally simply the heater consolidated with the filter pack. Water will go through the filter and will be warmed up in the meantime. You won't need to stress over additional pipes or holes.

What else do you require?

Thermostat: this will offer you some assistance with keeping the aquarium heat consistent.

Thermometer: aids you with monitoring the temperature of the aquarium water. It ought to likewise provide you some insight if the tank heater has fizzled or failed.

Spare heat radiator: this is your reinforcement. If your unique warmer falls flat, you need to ensure that you have another to put in immediately, or put the fish on stress.

Heater Guard: these fit over the warming component or element of a traditional radiator. They're typically made of plastic. It won't influence how the heater performs and has the additional advantage of guaranteeing that the fish don't blaze themselves on the unit when it gets hot. They're justified regardless of some measure of cash. In any case, they're justified irrespective of the cost. Presently, picking heaters and other tank temperature support gear shouldn't be so difficult.

Picking a Filtration System for Your Aquarium

Today's aquarium filters offer a wide assortment of choices to keep your aquarium water perfect and sound. While picking filtration, construct your choice on the size of your aquarium, and, also, the number of the fish, you would like to keep. To accomplish the most utterly awesome water conditions, you might need to utilize more than one kind of filter.

Air-driven Internal Filters

These little, modest box-like or froth filters are perfect for raising fry, healing facility or hospital aquariums, and few aquariums with small fish. They are sufficiently substantial to sustain excellent water conditions, yet sufficiently tender to keep little aquarium occupants free from damage. The vast majority of these gadgets give mechanical, compound, and organic filtration. These channels are put into the aquarium and permit you to find your aquarium near adjoining walls to spare space.

Under gravel filters

As their name recommends, these filters are set underneath a layer of aquarium rock. These filters move water through the rock to make conditions ideal for biological filtration. Once the useful microscopic organisms colonize the rock, they start to productively separate waste materials. Under gravel filters are economical and depend on either a vacuum apparatus or power head to work. Under gravel channels are natural channels. Be that as it may, many types highlight a replaceable cartridge set toward the end of the rigid tubing to give supplementary synthetic (actuated carbon) or mechanical (channel floss) filtration. These filters are accessible for little or vast aquariums yet are most appropriate for aquariums with a light fish load.

Inside Power Filters

Envision a power filter you can totally submerge. These helpful filters have the space-saving component of air-driven inside filters and the force and flexibility of standard force filters. These channels give fabulous water development and filtration since they are put close to the base of the aquarium. Waste items are removed before they have an opportunity to settle on the bottom of the aquarium. They are made for littler aquariums, for the most part under 20-gallons.

Power Filters

Power channels are presumably the most broadly utilized aquarium filters - and all things considered. They are anything but difficult to use and give astounding and perfect organic, mechanical and chemical filtration. The idea is to hang off the back of your aquarium and is the ideal filters for most popular aquarium sizes with an assortment of tropical fishes. Replaceable channel cartridges make upkeep straightforward and helpful. More up to date models highlight either an organic channel cushion or BIO-wheel to give additional contamination uprooting power.

Canister Filters

Canister filters provide prevalent mechanical, compound, and organic filtration for bigger aquariums or aquariums with a ton of fish. The "canister" or body bit of the filter is altogether more significant than most power filter - envision the whole amount of media canister filters can hold! Contingent upon the model, canister channels will have one to three (or all the more) large media wicker bin to hold diverse channel media sorts. Every media type is layered on top of one another to keep up incredible water quality. When contrasted with power filters, canister requires somewhat more push to set up and keep up. In any case, you will be astonished by their sifting power. These multipurpose channels are perfect for African and South American Cichlid aquariums, saltwater aquariums, and additionally freshwater planted aquariums.

Wet and Dry Filters

Wet and dry filters give a complete and fruitful organic filtration. They are extraordinary for saltwater fish-only aquariums or any huge aquarium setup that requires effective natural filtration. These channels are called wet and dry filters because the natural filter media is presented as air (dry) or aquarium water (wet). This outline makes the perfect environment for vast quantities of beneficial microbes to adequately prepare waste materials. When all is said and done, these aquarium filters require imagination put up. And this is because they should be introduced or plumbed to the aquarium in a somewhat technical way. Be that as it may, for the inventive and devoted aquarium specialist, setting up a wet or dry channel gives the perfect chance to develop a custom, stand-out filtration framework. Most models are intended for an arrangement under an aquarium and require a flood box (overflow) on the back. Most wet and dry filters incorporate a sump/supply (reservoir) that holds helper gear alongside the required water return pump.

Freshwater Aquarium Filters

Filtration is the critical process that will keep a freshwater aquarium clean and hospitable for all living organisms. Large bodies of water in the wild, like oceans and rivers, are able to dilute impurities, pollutants, and fish waste products in negligible amounts.

But with a freshwater aquarium, you are working with a smaller body of water that is constantly being recirculated. Pollutants need to be removed from this water on a regular basis so that the fish can stay happy and healthy.

There are three basic types of filtration necessary for a successful freshwater aquarium:

- Biological Filtration - Uses friendly bacteria to naturally remove nitrates from water.
- Mechanical Filtration - Removes particulate matter from freshwater by sieving out waste that floats in the water.
- Chemical Filtration - Removes waste and harmful chemicals by changing them into harmless compounds in the water.
- We need to have a filtration system big enough to handle the bio-load or the amount of animals in the aquarium.

Keep in mind that large, predatory fish are prone to eat more and produce more waste. A number of invertebrates are also more sensitive to nitrates than fish may be.

Different species of fish can withstand different amounts of waste in the water. This needs to be taken into account when setting up a filtration system.

The more filtration, the better. This is the case as long as the filtration is not stripping all good components out of the water.

The most basic and important way to keep your water clean is through the water change.

Make it your goal to change a quarter to a third of your water every two weeks. These regular water changes will help to keep the water cleaner, brighter, and happier. Your fish will become more active.

Regular water changes are one of the few ways that you can successfully reduce nitrate levels in the tank. While nitrate is not as toxic as nitrite or ammonia, it is not the best thing to have in your tank. When nitrate reaches certain levels, it can become toxic. Nitrate is a great fertilizer that encourages algae to grow, which is something that should be avoided in a freshwater tank.

When changing the water, you can't simply do one water change. You must do two small water changes, or else you will upset the balance of the tank and put your fish in danger. A healthy aquarium will not move quickly, so you must be patient in this process. Only bad things happen overnight.

Biological Filtration

I talked about the nitrification cycle earlier, which allows you to take advantage of friendly bacteria in the tank to metabolize nitrates right out of the water.

When I first began my aquarium, I did not know that this was what was keeping my aquarium in balance. I thought that if I made my aquarium as close to a natural habitat as possible with adequate filtration, then everything would be fine.

What I had done was create a balance of gravel and sand in the substrate to host bacteria. Bacteria had also colonized the pad in my filter. At first, I thought that the plants were absorbing all of the waste of the aquarium, but it was actually the friendly bacteria doing this work for me.

Good bacteria will grow in the substrate, on the tank, and on any decorations. When they have proper oxygen and ammonia, they will be there at all times to break down nitrates and nitrites.

Mechanical Filtration

If you examine your aquarium, you may see tiny floating particles, and there are also many particles that you are not able to see. If you look at the base of some tank decorations and in the corners of the tank, you will see detritus - a brown or grey matter. This is what your mechanical filters are removing from the aquarium.

This is removed using a filter that has small holes to trap the floating waste particles. This occurs using filter floss, a plastic bio-mat that will provide a surface for bacteria to grow. Many times, particulate filters will also come as a sponge or cartridge.

Sponges and plastic mats will be reusable for a period of time. Cartridges often clog up, so they may need to be removed. Many people use sand beds and gravel in trickle or wet and dry filters.

Another type of mechanical filtration works with a foam-fracturing device, known as a protein skimmer. This is a method used in human water treatment, where a stream of small bubbles is injected directly into a column of water.

This will create foam to capture microscopic particles outside of the fine bubbles that overflow into a holding cup. Many people worry that this system will also remove trace elements like strontium and iodine at the same time.

It is my personal belief that the advantages of this filtration system far outweigh the risk. If you're concerned about trace elements, you should be using trace element supplements anyway. You can also use less advanced technology like a siphon or scoop to remove detritus from the tank.

Chemical Filtration

Chemical filtration is used to remove chemicals that have dissolved in the water. The most popular and widely used method is with activated charcoal. Keep in mind that this is not using ordinary charcoal; the charcoal has been heated to a high temperature using steam. The charcoal will then develop millions of tiny pores that open up in the heat.

Charcoal is carbon, which will bond to other chemicals. In a freshwater aquarium, carbon will become a chemical sponge to trap and remove heavy metals, pollutants, and waste. Carbon removes any chemicals that cause water discoloration, like tannins and other compounds that can give water an unpleasant odor.

It is far better to use an activated carbon that is low in phosphate.

Charcoal is made from coal, which is compressed fossilized plant matter. This means that charcoal will contain a large amount of phosphate, which causes algae to grow. This is something that you want to avoid in your freshwater aquarium.

Charcoal is ideal because it is inexpensive and beneficial. However, it doesn't provide a substitute for biological filtration, and it should not be used as a filter media for that purpose. Many people are concerned that carbon will remove trace elements in planted aquarium settings, which are required for healthy growth.

But you should be replacing these chemicals anyway with supplementation, so a carbon filter should not cause any issues. Carbon filtration has so many advantages that, when you use it with a good supplement, it will not cause a problem. Make sure to thoroughly wash the dust off of the carbon so that the water in your tank does not turn black from a coating of coal dust.

You are also able to purchase additives like "ammo-lock" and "phos-guard" to name two. "Ammo-lock" and it's like are useful in emergencies, but you really shouldn't have these type of problems anyway. "Ammo-lock" uses salts to bind with the highly soluble nitrates and render them into less harmful chemicals.

Things like "phos-guard" are useful too in problem situations, like removing phosphate. You can buy products to remove almost every conceivable chemical from the water. It is better, however, to find out why it is there and how to get rid of the cause.

Filter Technology

There are a number of different filters that range from air pump driven corner filters to elaborate systems with wet and dry trickles, fluidized sand beds, and large capacity skimming capabilities. There are as many filter variations as there are companies that make the filters, and each will claim that theirs is the best. Some filters will definitely work better than others.

For example, a corner box filter that has a small sponge is easy and inexpensive. It filters well, but it is unattractive and takes up too much space in a tank. The filter that you choose will come down to personal preference.

There is no real formula to determine how big a filter you should use. If you are buying a power filter or a canister, check out specific manufacturer's directions beforehand.

The basic rule here is the bigger the filter, the better.

Power Filters

The first type of filter that I ever purchased was a power filter. A power filter is easy to care for and is generally out of the way in a tank.

A power filter will hang at the back of a tank and pull water in through a tube using an impeller. It will then push the water back out through a carbon cartridge for high quality filtration.

The "Penguin Power Filter" from Marineland Aquarium Products

The cartridge is a particulate filter that has a good surface area for healthy bacteria growth. The carbon in the filter will offer chemical filtration.

The disadvantage is that the cartridges do not last as long and can be somewhat expensive. It is possible to set up a mat, floss sponge, or regular sponge within these filters yourself to save money, although it will not provide activated charcoal filtration.

In a smaller tank, this should not pose an issue. You can always place an old stocking with a small amount of charcoal in it behind the filter overflow. Some larger filters offer this addition without the stocking, which will make it much more convenient. You will need to clean the floss, mat, and sponge on a regular basis. Otherwise, trapped waste will begin to decompose within the water, and the filter will not remove waste properly.

Canister Filters

Jebo Aquarium External Canister Filter

Canister filters are normally sold with beginner freshwater setups. They are ideal since they are easy to operate, and they work efficiently. Canister filters work as a large power filter in their basic function.

They are located underneath the tank; they siphon in and pull out water using different media types. They will then pump the water directly back into the tank.

These filters provide great mechanical and bacterial filtration. They have a high flow rate, which means that they can filter a large volume of water adequately. They use different types of media.

Many filters use ceramic rings or sintered glass, which provide a large surface area but must eventually be replaced when they are exhausted.

The filters may also use limestone chips to buffer the water and provide a larger surface area for bacteria to grow. The water may be passed through a number of different matching grates that will trap particles. The filters are overall very easy to use and remain clean; they are self-contained, compact, and simple to care for.

You do have to keep the filters clean regularly, similarly to power filters, in order to avoid particulate waste decomposition within the filter. These are ideal beginner filters from my own personal experience, but when you move onto a larger tank, you may need to look at other alternatives, like trickle filters.

Under gravel Filters

Under gravel filters are normally sold in beginner packages because they are highly efficient and cheap. They suck water with an air lifter powerhead directly from the tank to the substrate, which sits on top of a plastic grate.

The substrate works through filtration media, which will provide you with a larger surface area to work with. Undergravel filters work well as biological filters, but they do have a number of disadvantages. Most aquarium enthusiasts today consider undergravel filters to be outdated.

Gravel will clog the filter with debris and increase the flow rate over time, which will decrease filtration. This will cause waste build-up in the water to greatly reduce water quality. Water flow is restricted through the gravel. This will create anaerobic pockets and promote the breeding of harmful bacteria, which could pollute a tank.

Undergravel filters are prone to clogging, even if you vacuum the surface regularly. They do not work well as mechanical filters because particulate waste gets quickly trapped in the substrate.

This will create a strain on the biological filtration when matter decomposes. The more that is filtered, the more clogged the filter will become. This will greatly reduce the flow rate of water in the filter, which will affect tank filtration for the worse.

When the substrate becomes completely clogged, you will not have a filter and will be left with a large amount of detritus decomposing in the bottom of the tank. When this occurs, you have to take the tank apart completely to clean the substrate and filter. In a large tank, this is something that you want to avoid at all costs.

The undergravel filter can be run in reverse, which will push water through the substrate. Your powerhead will require a prefilter so that it does not become blocked and burn out. As you can see, there are a number of reasons that undergravel filters are no longer recommended for freshwater aquariums.

Trickle Filters

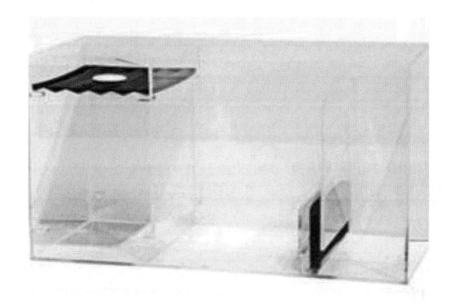

A trickle filter may also be known as a wet/dry filter. This filter will work by allowing water to trickle through different layers of media to expose both media and water to the air for higher oxygenation. A trickle filter can even be created from a modified set of plastic drawers if you can find a set in a suitable size.

A stack of boxes will also work well if you are making your own filter. Your tank will need a large enough overflow and sump - a big box or tank underneath the tank to hold water. The overflow should flow into a prefilter of floss, matting, or foam.

SeaClear Vanguard Wet/Dry Trickle Filter

The water will flow into different levels of the trickle filter. Some filters use rotating spray bars, but these are more expensive filters that are prone to malfunction if the holes become blocked or corroded. A simple drip tray is best and can be created by drilling small holes into the bottom of a tray on each layer.

The filter should flow at a medium intensity so that it does not wash bacteria from the media; this will give the water time to come into contact with the media. You can use many different things for your media, such as limestone chips, bio balls, sintered glass rings, or a carbon layer for chemical filtration.

As the layers are exposed to water, it is best to have one layer that is completely submerged in the bottom of the sump. This will create anaerobic de-nitrification to remove excess nitrates. I personally love trickle filters because you can add many types of media to create one large, "superfilter" device.

Protein Skimmers

Hydor Slim-Skim Protein Skimmer

One drawback of these filters is that you will lose a lot of water due to evaporation, so watch your water level.

Protein skimmers were originally used to treat sewage. This is a technology that has now been used to clean out water for aquariums. Protein skimmers are beneficial gadgets because they clean organic waste before the good bacteria in a tank can do their job.

Protein skimmers will mechanically remove tiny nitrates that may pollute the water before they can be broken down by biological systems. This will help to keep the water clean and improve the efficiency of all filtration in a tank.

This happens because organic chemicals get caught in the surface tension in bubbles. They will serve as microscopic mechanical filters that remove tiny particles from the surface of the bubbles as they are skimmed from the column of water.

However, in a freshwater tank, this skimming will not be effective unless you have a high pH and a higher specific gravity.

Still, your water quality can be increased dramatically by using a protein skimmer. When using a protein skimmer, it is important to remember to use trace element supplements!

There are a few types of protein skimmers, and they work in many different ways, but they all rely upon the same principle of foam fractioning.

The two most common are the venturi and airstone driven skimmers.

The airstone driven skimmer is, as its name implies, driven by air. Air is driven through a cork or glass airstone (specially designed so as to have a small and dense enough formation of air bubbles) by a diaphragm air pump. These bubbles flow up the column of water, producing foam on the top and capturing the organic compounds.

Venturi skimmers use a venturi valve, which is a special type of valve that draws air in through the valve, injecting it into a stream of moving water. This then allows the bubbles to rise from the bottom of the water column, where the stream is injected, and a foam fraction forms.

When choosing a protein skimmer, it's good to know a few important points before you go and splash out on one. For starters, they are pricey for what they are - essentially a cylinder of plastic with some kind of pump attached to it.

With the basic air pump driven protein skimmer, you will need spare air stones. These are specific for skimmers and not your ordinary decorative air stones. You need to replace these about every month or two as they lose their integrity, and they will not produce bubbles of the correct diameter.

Air driven skimming is gentler on plankton and the unfortunate side effect of removing trace elements from the water. It is also more temperamental and fiddly to set up and maintain.

Venturi skimmers have their own problems, however. They need good, strong high flow pumps to power the skimming action. They are usually more expensive, and they might also require you to buy the pump on top of the skimmer's price, depending on the particular setup.

Lights

Lighting in a tank has two main purposes. It enables you to see your fish, and it provides vital energy for plants. In order to grow plants, you need special lights that provide the correct intensity and spectrum.

Normal incandescent lights or light globes do not provide the right spectrum of light for plants and are not bright enough. They tend to run hot, which will alter the temperature of your water.

In a freshwater aquarium, there are several different options regarding lighting. If you are keeping fish with very little plant growth, you can use fluorescent tubes that provide a full light spectrum. There are many manufacturers like Phillips and Hagen that produce light globes.

You will be able to find a selection at your local aquarium shop. These lights will be available as High Output or Very High Output. You will first of all want daylight or full-spectrum tubes, such as the Osram Lumilux or LIFE GLO tubes.

Coralife Freshwater Lunar Aqualight

The lights in an aquarium should be mounted in a light hood or mounting. You can purchase inexpensive units from a local aquarium shop. The units will consist of a fluorescent tube mounting unit, a ballast unit connecting a cable to the lighting mount, and a power cable.

If you are handy with a soldering iron and are confident in playing with electricity, you can easily construct it yourself. The mounts for the aquarium are no different, except they have a box around the starting fixture. Go and have a look at what you can buy, and then check out your local electrician's supplies. It will be quite cheaper to make this than spend the premium to have "aquarium" slapped on the side. Then you can go and purchase your globes.

If you have plant growth, you will not only want full spectrum tubes but some tubes that provide extra boost to the spectrums that make plants grow. These will be galled "gro plus", "gro-lux, "super grow" - you get the idea. These will help your plants photosynthesize that bit extra.

They will also be HO and VHO.

You will want 4 watts per gallon (1 watt per litre) of water when it comes to working out how much light you need, with a mixture of extra growing lights and full spectrum lights.

If your tank does not have plants, you will need about 1 watt per gallon (every five litres) or so. If you don't have the plants to take up the light and nutrients, algae will grow. So make sure your tanks water is free from nitrates.

Furthermore, if you want your plants to die and to grow lots of algae in your tank, use normal household fluorescents. They are totally the incorrect spectrum of light and the wrong intensity. All fluorescents will have lost their proper output of their spectrum after about nine to twelve months; some people replace them every three to six months. This can get expensive, and I've never seen the need to if they are working okay.

There is also a shift towards using power compact units. These are similar to fluorescents, except small and stronger; they don't get as hot, and they generally keep their spectrum better.

You should leave your main lights on for around eight to ten hours.

Substrate

The substrate has multiple purposes. The first is to serve as part of the filtration, especially if you happen to use an undergravel filter. The substrate will also act as part of the tank décor and provide a place for plants to grow in a freshwater tank.

Your fish's colours will be affected by the colour of your substrate.

If your substrate is dark, the colours of your fish will be much deeper to blend into the colour of the substrate. If you use coloured gravel, the dyes may leach into the water, which is unhealthy for your fish. I personally do not prefer the look of coloured gravel, but it is a personal decision.

You can use gravel or sand for your substrate. Be careful with the type of gravel that you choose since not all minerals in rocks will be inert, meaning that they could leach toxic compounds into your aquarium.

The best way to find out if gravel will leach carbonates into the water is to drop a small amount of vinegar on the surface. If the vinegar bubbles, the gravel will leach carbonates.

It is even better to allow gravel to sit in a bucket of water to determine what the pH is after one week. Wash and stir the gravel in the bucket, and wash it again before you place it in the tank to remove dust or silt.

A dark colour substrate may bring out brighter colours in your fish, but a lighter colour offers a more natural look in the habitat. This again depends upon the setting of your aquarium.

Powerheads

A powerhead is a pump that is totally submerged in a tank. It is necessary to create high flow in the water.

In all freshwater tanks, you want the surface to be agitated to provide a good oxygen transfer between the air and the surface of the water. Powerheads can also drive undergravel filters and help pump water in and out of your tank.

Powerheads are handy gadgets but can often stop working without any notice. Make sure that you always have a spare on hand to avoid any potential problems.

Without adequate circulation, your aquarium will have what are called dead spots, which could create instability in the water.

These dead spots will also feed large amounts of algae. But remember that if your powerhead is too powerful, it will create a small storm in your aquarium.

Two smaller powerheads are much better than one enormous one.

800 GPH Powerhead Aquarium Pump Wave Maker

Second Hand Equipment

Second hand equipment is cheap and convenient to find. But when buying second hand, you must check everything that you purchase for quality. Don't even think about trying to fix a broken glass tank if you are new to aquariums. The time, effort, and energy that you spend will not be worth it. You should buy a new one instead.

Check specifically for strong seals and scratches in any second hand tank. Put the tank out in your garage and fill it completely with tap water for several days so that any leaks will present themselves. Make sure that you place the tank on a sheet of polystyrene so that its weight is evenly distributed if it is not level.

Older heaters and pumps will likely be less functional the older that they get. You might be lucky and find a pump or heater that will still have several good years left. Protein skimmers are generally good second hand, as long as they have clear valves with replaceable pumps.

Care of the aquarium

The fish and plants are doing well. Everything has developed magnificently. You enjoy looking at your little underwater world. But this alone is not enough. To keep it that way, care is necessary. Some things are done quickly, others take longer. And perhaps there will also be one or two things that you won't like so much, because you might have imagined it quite differently. In such moments just think about the beautiful aquarium and how great everything has developed. You see, everything is not so bad.

Feeding

People like to do this and it is always exciting to watch. But here applies, less is more. You should find a good compromise, so that on the one hand all animals are fed and on the other hand no food is left lying around. The food that is left lying around pollutes the water and can be the cause of poor water quality. You remember the bacteria that convert waste into nitrite? Therefore, it is better to feed sparingly. Also, you will have more time to watch.

You should know your inhabitants and accordingly have suitable food in stock. There are certainly fish that need to be fed very specifically. Not only the type of food, but also the way of feeding. Therefore, inform absolutely before purchase of the animals exactly about the conditions!

With these mentioned animals usually the usual and widespread flake food and food tablets for the bottom dwellers are sufficient. However, even here you have to take into account whether it is a carnivore or vegetarian and choose the appropriate product accordingly. But we humans also do not want to eat the same thing every day. Therefore, it can also be worthwhile to deal more extensively with the topic of food and to bring variety to the menu. Your animals will thank you with health and more beautiful colors. Beside flake food there is also frozen food in the trade, which is also easy to feed. You can make the menu even more interesting by growing the fish food yourself. In the form of microorganisms, such as water fleas or Artemia. However, you can deal with this topic later. Ready-made food is sufficient for the beginning.

Gardening

This is likely to be the maintenance work that is the most time consuming. Again, of course, it depends a lot on the amount of plants you have. But if your plants are growing well, you can expect to have to cut back some plants every two weeks. If the tank is too overgrown, it usually doesn't look nice either and the fish still want some swimming space too. So get out the sharp scissors and go. But how and where?

The easiest way is with stem plants. You can simply cut them off at the top and you can even stick the head back into the ground. After a short time it will grow roots again and you will have a new plant. If the plant is no longer so beautiful at the bottom, you can also replace the unsightly part in this way so. But that then not with all plants at the same time, that could bring your stable biotope again out of balance.

With the Amazon sword plant it can happen that it grows too high or also becomes too powerful in the width and takes away space or light from other smaller plants. Then you should cut off a few leaves as close to the ground as possible. You can also propagate this plant. It quite often forms shoots on which small daughter plants are formed. You can plant these as soon as roots have grown.

Mosses or grass-like plants spread all by themselves and form a dense carpet over time. But this usually requires a lot of light for them to grow compactly and regular pruning, and you can also replant the cut plantlets in the ground. However, this can be a test of patience, since the small plants hardly find a foothold as long as there are no roots.

Water Change

Our biotope is well run in and yet it remains an artificially created biotope, which does not exist in the wild. As well as the metabolic cycle works, it comes in most aquariums sooner or later to the point that some substances can not be degraded. And then they remain in the aquarium and the time comes when the biotope is no longer stable or the animals are not doing so well and may even die. To prevent this, the pollutants must be regularly removed from the aquarium. The easiest way to do this is to change the water. The emphasis here is clearly on regular. 30% of the water volume every two weeks is sufficient. This is not much and, depending on the size of the aquarium, can be done quite quickly. Ideally, you can combine this directly with the bottom cleaning and at the same time the next maintenance task is done. For small and medium aquariums, you simply take a short hose, one end you hold in the bucket, which is slightly lower than the aquarium. The other end goes into the aquarium. Now suck once briefly and vigorously on the hose end in the bucket and the water runs from the aquarium into the bucket. Almost all by itself. Just make sure that no fish or other inhabitants are transported into the bucket. Otherwise, they have to get out of the bucket and into the aquarium again, which can be tedious with the landing net. If one has the 30% out, they must also again purely. The easiest way to do this is with the bucket. Get fresh water from the tap and pour it carefully into the aquarium. But if the aquarium is larger, then the bucket can quickly become laborious, because you may have to run 10 times or even more. Here you can proceed according to the same principle, but with a long water hose directly to the bathroom. However, due to the length of the hose, the flow rate may be slower and the water change alone may be longer. But you save yourself some running around and lugging buckets.

As already mentioned, it is quite good to do a regular water change with not too much water. But sometimes you have to deviate from the rule. This is necessary if the nitrate value has suddenly risen or other pollutants contaminate the water. This puts our inhabitants in danger and a large water change is urgently necessary. In this case even up to 90%. Until the water values are stable again in the safe range, this may even be necessary several times a day. But this is not the rule and should not scare you off! A small tip! You do not need to throw away the aquarium water. As watering water, for indoor or garden plants, it is perfectly suitable.

Bottom Cleaning

Like any animal, a fish or shrimp will eventually excrete its food. And this then collects together with other waste, such as leaves or food remains on the bottom. The so-called mum. With coarse gravel it falls into the gaps and is not noticed so quickly. But with fine sand, especially with light-colored types, you can see the mum very quickly, because it remains on top. Due to the current in the aquarium, the stuff also likes to collect in several places. Now one can say, this is not so bad and belongs to it. Precisely because this is also the food basis for important bacteria. But it becomes then nevertheless times too much and can then also the water unnecessarily load. That's why we're taking the stuff out now. We don't have to be too thorough. It is enough to free the worst corners. As just described in the chapter before, you can do this directly during the water change. There one is anyway already with the hands in the water. But there are also a few tools to make the work a little easier. So-called mud vacuum cleaner is connected to the end of the hose in the aquarium and allow a particularly thorough cleaning deep into the bottom. Is actually not necessary and makes only with gravel really sense, because the tiny grains of sand are much too light and thus stirred up and also sucked off. This is clearly too much of a good thing. Some systems offer a suction function that saves you from having to suck with your mouth. This can be useful for people who shy away from mouth contact. You can do this, but it is absolutely unfounded for health reasons. Beyond mulch bells, there are proper battery-powered vacuum cleaners. These devices promise a simple floor cleaning - without water change. However, due to their design, they cannot develop a strong suction power and you usually need more patience for cleaning the bottom. But for small aquariums it can be quite suitable.

Filter Cleaning

In my opinion, the filter is the only device that is a bit more complicated to maintain. And here, the smaller the filter and the more stock in the aquarium, the more often you have to clean it. But that's not witchcraft either. A small rule in advance, you should not clean the filter on the same day as the water change is done. This could cause too many bacteria to disappear from the aquarium at once, and we need them.

The small internal filters are usually only foam sponges or cartridges. Depending on the manufacturer, you can rinse them briefly under lukewarm running water or simply replace them with a new one. The larger external filters are more complex. However, even here everything is rinsed only with lukewarm water. Here it is only important that you assemble everything in the reverse order to how you disassembled it. When to clean the filter? Some manufacturers specify a cleaning cycle. However, I keep it very simple. If the flow rate has decreased significantly or the water is no longer filtered clearly, then the filter should be cleaned. By the way, the hoses of the external filter do not have to be cleaned every time. Deposits also settle here, but experience has shown that it takes much longer until the flow is prevented.

Pane Cleaning

The frequency of glass cleaning depends more on the growth of algae. If there is little algae in the aquarium, then there is also less coating on the panes and it must be ensured less often for clear view.

If it should be necessary, there are different possibilities. Very classical are magnetic cleaners. A part equipped with smooth felt or fabric remains on the outside and a part equipped with rough material is placed on the inside of the pane in the aquarium. If you now move the outer part, the counterpart on the inside also does it and eliminates the algae. You can also leave this solution in the aquarium and quickly „go over"it if necessary. But you should avoid getting into the bottom at all costs. If a stone or grain of sand gets between the magnets, scratches can no longer be avoided! By the way, floating magnets prevent wet hands when fishing out again.

As alternatives, there are countless sponges on offer or disc cleaners with razor blades. The latter are very effective and are available on a long rod, so that you do not have to use your hands in the water. In the variant with the razor blades, however, it is important to work carefully so that no scratches come into the glass and especially the silicone seams are not injured. But as long as you slowly put the razor blade always straight on, nothing happens.

From the outside, you can also clean the windows from time to time. This is easily done with a damp cloth and then with a dry, non-fluffy cloth. There is also nothing against a glass cleaner, as long as nothing of it gets into the aquarium.

Diseases

Unfortunately, fish can also become ill. There it goes to the animals quite similarly as us humans. But honestly, the diseases of humans are better researched and also better treatable. Especially with small fishes one usually has little time to do anything at all. It is also difficult to always find a reason why a fish died. In any case you should measure the water values in this case. So you can at least exclude that a water value has slipped into a dangerous range. And other animals are also in danger.

However, if several fish show the same symptom, or even just a single one, then the best thing to do is to set up a small sick bay and quarantine the sick candidates for the time being. This means, of course, that you have to set up a separate aquarium. It doesn't have to be that big and it doesn't have to be overgrown. But you should have thought in advance where you can set up such a sick bay for a short time. It is important to note that you fill the infirmary with water from the main aquarium. The small tanks are usually operated with small internal filters. This can be run in the large tank a few hours before. Then a few bacteria have already settled there. You can do without plants and substrate for the time being. In this tank you can now take a close look at the patient and then consult specialist literature. You can also try a specialized store. But then please in a real one. Nothing against hardware stores, but usually only salesmen are employed there. In a specialized store the chance is higher to meet an experienced aquarist. They have their own experience with one or the other diseases and medications. In the accessories there is a whole range of medications for various diseases. Most of the treatments require isolation of the patients and it is highly advisable to stick to the given dosage. And here, too, then usually helps only patience and hope.

Safety Tips

Some of these safety tips for handling your aquarium may be common sense, but they're still worth being said...

- Only use devices that are made for freshwater aquariums.
- Only use electrical devices that are UL listed, meaning that they are regulated by the Underwriters Laboratory. The Underwriters Laboratory is a product safety certification organization that has been in business since 1894. UL has developed strict standards for products, assemblies, and materials regarding product safety. Electronics that are UL certified have met product safety requirements so that all electrical components can be used as directed without posing any risk or harm to the user.
- Try to use electrical outlets that are GFIC equipped. A GFCI outlet is a ground-fault circuit interrupter outlet that protects from electrical shock. A GFCI will monitor the amount of current that flows from hot to neutral in an appliance. If there's an imbalance in electricity, the circuit will be tripped within 1/30 of a second to protect against electrical shock in the case of a malfunction. These electrical outlets have a reset

button that must be set each time the electricity surges or goes out.

- Hang power cords below the outlet before running them up to your tank. This will ensure that any water that drips down the cord will not run directly into the electrical outlet.
- Keep the aquarium stand to one side of an electrical outlet to reduce the chance of cords getting wet.
- Unplug all electrical cords any time you maintain the tank, including changing the water.
- If any electrical equipment falls into the tank, don't automatically reach for it before unplugging it!
- Inspect your equipment on a regular basis and replace any worn or broken parts.

Conclusion

A freshwater aquarium is a type of aquarium in which the fish, plants, and other organisms have no special requirements regarding salinity. While marine fish can tolerate a wide range of salinity, freshwater fish need a specific range of salinity to thrive. Aquarium plants have varying tolerances to different water chemistry parameters such as hardness (dH), alkalinity (KH), and pH.

An aquarium is a tank or an artificial pond where fish, plants, and other aquatic organisms are kept. Fish keepers use this aquatic habitat to keep fish, plants, and invertebrates for their enjoyment, for shelter, or to study their behavior. There are freshwater and marine aquariums. They have become popular in recent decades with the availability of specialized equipment such as heaters and filters.

A freshwater aquarium is a type of vivarium made to house freshwater aquatic animals. The term generally refers to a tank or an aquarium with liquid and solid materials. Freshwater fish are often sold as food for larger fish, reptiles, or amphibians.

Freshwater fish are being kept in aquariums all over the world for several reasons. Their beauty and grace is part of the reason why many people love to have them as pets. Freshwater aquarium fish are also easy to care for as long as you know what exactly to do. It also doesn't hurt that there are a wide variety of freshwater fish to choose from.

Now, if you're thinking of getting into aquariums, I hope this has been a good primer. If you've already got experience in this hobby, maybe some of the information here will be new to you. Either way, I hope you've enjoyed reading the book and if you end up setting up your own aquarium, I hope it flows as well as mine has.

Printed in Poland
by Amazon Fulfillment
Poland Sp. z o.o., Wrocław